Vijaya Kumar

NEW DAWN PRESS, INC.
Chicago • Slough • New Delhi

NEW DAWN PRESS GROUP

Published by New Dawn Press Group
New Dawn Press, Inc., 244 South Randall Rd # 90, Elgin, IL 60123
New Dawn Press, 2 Tintern Close, Slough, Berkshire, SL1-2TB, UK
New Dawn Press (An Imprint of Sterling Publishers (P) Ltd.)
A-59, Okhla Industrial Area, Phase-II, New Delhi-110020

A Little Book of Feng Shui
Copyright © 2004, New Dawn Press
ISBN 1 932705 12 0

NOTE FROM THE PUBLISHER

*The author specifically disclaims any liability, loss or risk
whatsoever, which is incurred or likely to be incurred, as
a consequence of any direct or indirect use of information
given in this book. The contents of this work are a
personal interpretation of the subject by the author.*

PRINTED IN INDIA

Contents

Preface

This books is by no means an extensive study by any professional. The data provided in this book are my own interpretations of the subject, gleaned from various books, and presented from a layperson's viewpoint.

The book deals with each aspect of the study, point by point, in a simple language, and serves as a ready reckoner for those who have no time to go through heavy, indepth studies.

The publishers and I hold no responsibility for any discrepancy in the script. We would welcome suggestions or intimation of errors that come to anybody's notice.

Vijaya Kumar

Introduction

Feng Shui literally means 'wind' and 'water', respectively. It is an ancient Chinese art of creating harmonious surroundings to bring one happiness, prosperity and good health.

The Chinese strongly believe that environmental forces, like wind and water, should be ideally positioned in the universe to enhance the balance of nature. The Yin-Yang concept of the Chinese links nature with man, and governs the universe.

The ch'i, or cosmic force, is the most important principle of Feng Shui. The ch'i pervading every nook of the universe helps plants and crops to grow and flourish, brings harmony within society, and moves within the body as *prana* or life-force.

Feng Shui provides necessary knowledge in planning a building, and its internal environment.

Feng Shui — Meaning

1. Feng Shui is an ancient Chinese art which had its origin in India during Buddha's existence.

2. It is a system which links man and his fate to his surroundings.

3. It helps in bringing health, wealth and happiness.

4. It gives us guidance as to how we can alter our surroundings in order to bring harmony into our life.

5. It provides necessary information on suitable decor for the house.

6. It also helps in the selection of the right colour scheme for the house, flat, shop, etc.

7. It provides useful information about our internal environment, suggesting how to control the forces affecting them.

8. All constructions, including entrances, staircase, lofts, etc., are designed according to the Feng Shui rules.

10. By altering the location of a bed or a table, one can either block or enhance the flow of ch'i.

11. By interpreting the hidden, mysterious forces of the cosmos, Feng Shui provides a practical approach to environmental planning.

12. The Feng Shui environment falls into two categories — physical and directional.

13. The physical environment refers to the visible features around us, like mountains, buildings, rivers, roads, trees, etc., each wielding some influence by their position in relation to the house, shop, etc.

14. The directional environment is invisible and are either magnetic waves or cosmic rays and energy which can be harnessed for beneficial gains.

15. Where no alternative changes can be made to a building, basic cures like mirror, flutes, colours, wind chime, etc., can be applied.

Yin and Yang

1. Taoism is the religion of China, and the word 'Tao' means 'The Way'.

2. Tao is the process linking man and the universe.

3. Tao is referred to as the 'Great Ultimate'.

4. Out of Tao comes the yin and yang, the complementary forces that govern the universe.

5. Tao, or the Great Ultimate, generates yang through movements, and it becomes tranquil when its activity reaches the zenith.

6. The Great Ultimate generates the yin through tranquillity.

7. Thus the alternating movement and tranquillity establish the yin and the yang.

8. With the union of yin and yang, the five elements of earth, water, fire, wood and metal arise.

9. With the distribution of these material forces in a balanced and harmonious way, the four seasons follow in a cycle.

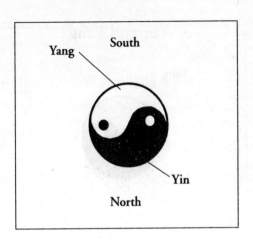

Yin and Yang

10. Yin is feminine, passive and dark.

11. Yang is masculine, active and light.

12. These opposite forces always contain an element of each other. A minute dot of yang is always present in the dark yin, and vice versa.

13. Yin and yang are dependant on each other.

14. The light yang represents summer and south, while dark yin represents winter and north.

15. The light yang is always at the top, while the dark yin is always at the bottom for all

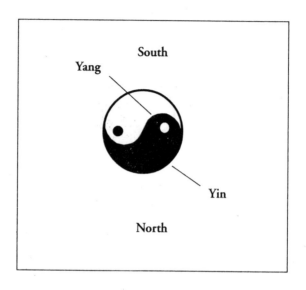

South

Yang

Yin

North

Chinese compasses have south at the top, and north at the bottom.

16. Yin, representing earth, is denoted by broken lines and a square, whereas yang, representing heaven, is indicated by a solid unbroken line, and a circle.

17. Yin and Yang pervade everything in different proportions.

18. To ensure harmony, a balance between the two is essential.

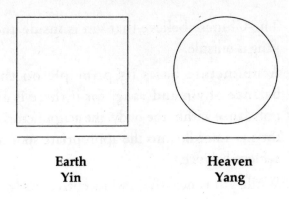

Earth
Yin

Heaven
Yang

For example, the walls of an office room can have a warm colour, whereas the furniture can be of a cool colour.

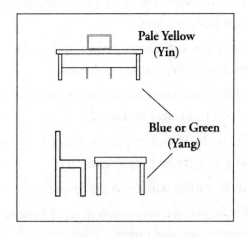

Pale Yellow
(Yin)

Blue or Green
(Yang)

Balance of Yin and Yang

19. The Chinese believe that yin is inside and yang is outside.

20. Acupuncture bases its principle on the balance of yin and yang, for if there is an imbalance within the body, the acupuncturist thrusts a needle into the appropriate spot to achieve balance.

21. While yin is negative and receptive, yang is positive and creative.

22. Yin is a yielding follower, whereas yang is a strong leader.

23. Yin is attributed with a heavy body, while yang has a buoyant soul.

24. While yin represents action and matter, yang represents inspiration and spirit.

25. While yin is shadow, and is wet and soft, yang is sun, and is dry and hard.

26. Yin is dark and represents night, where as yang is light and represents day.

27. Yin is secular while yang is divine.

28. While yin denotes down, and inner, yang denotes up, and outer.

Ch'i

1. Ch'i, known as *prana* in India, is the cosmic breath or life-force.

2. Ch'i is the essential principle of Feng Shui.

3. It is the essential breath that maintains physical, emotional and environmental balance.

4. It links the mind with matter, conveying not only the message, say, to move, but also moves us.

5. It also links man with his surroundings.

6. It creates a process of flowing quickly and standing still, flourishing and decaying, increasing and decreasing, etc.

7. Ch'i, moving through a room, creates a pleasant and conducive atmosphere, thereby also energising the room.

8. Mirrors in a room help in ch'i being reflected back and forth, thus enlivening a room.

9. Ch'i never leaves by the door it has entered, so it is always better to ensure that all doors

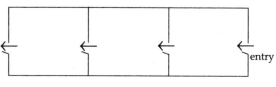

Chi's entry and exit

open in the direction of the flow. Ch'i can then go from one room to another before going out.

10. Where a room has no window, and has only one door, ch'i circulates in the room and becomes stagnant.

11. Live ch'i generates energy, while the dead one arrests growth.

12. When yin and yang are balanced, ch'i is live and energetic, and it is a dead ch'i which enters a room if yin and yang are imbalanced.

   For Example, it is not advisable to have a bedroom over a garage which has only one door, and is mostly always closed, thereby harbouring a dead ch'i.

13. When ch'i, after breathing life into a certain area, disperses and decays, it allows sha, the opposite of ch'i, to enter.

16

14. Sha is a negative force which hovers over stagnant water or poorly drained soil.

15. Arising from the earth, or pervading cold and sharp winds, it penetrates protective walls, hedges, etc.

16. Another type of sha that travels in straight lines along rivers, railway lines, telephone lines, etc., can be arrested by fences, rows of trees, etc.

17. Sha affects landscapes as well as one's health when it accumulates over an area.

18. Ch'i which is benefic, moves slowly in gentle curves, while sha, being malefic, rushes in harsh straight lines.

The Elements

1. Five elements control and govern all things in this universe.
2. The five basic elements are wood, fire, earth, water and metal, which are essential for the Feng Shui system.
3. They channelise and harmonise the ch'i of the individual and his/her environment.
4. Each of these elements is blessed with a definite colour, season, and direction.
5. The strength of these elements changes with the seasons.

Element	Direction	Colour	Season
Wood	East	Green	Spring
Fire	South	Red	Summer
Earth	Centre	Yellow	—
Water	North	Black	Winter
Metal	West	White	Autumn

The Elements and their Associations

6. Wood signifies growth in a plant, and all plants prosper in spring.
7. Fire is most prosperous in summer when the sun is hottest.

8. The earth's central element is neutral, and as such, its presence is felt all through the year.

9. Water, associated with ice and snow, becomes stronger in the cold winter.

10. During autumn, when the wood is weak and leaves fall, metal becomes stronger.

11. These elements, influencing each other, create and destroy each other in fixed succession.

12. All elements, grouped together and influencing each other, work in cycles.

    For example, fire produces earth in the form of ash.

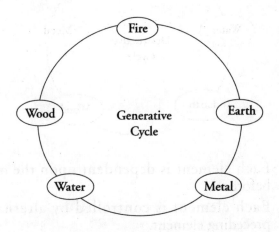

Earth produces metal in the form of Minerals
Metal produces water.
Water produces wood.
Wood produces fire.

13. All alternate elements destroy each other.
    For example, earth pollutes water.
    Water extinguishes fire.
    Fire melts metal.
    Metal cuts wood.
    Wood harms earth.

Destructive Cycle

14. Each element is dependent upon the one before it.
15. Each element is controlled by alternate preceding element.

For example, in a green painted room, with all furnishing and flooring in green, the person living in it will spend most of his time in imagination, removed from pragmatism. A cure for this would be to have white or red furniture or carpet or furnishings. White (the colour of metal) cuts green (the colour of wood) and thus balances the effect, while red (the colour of fire) harmonises the room, for wood produces fire.

16. The shape of all things— buildings, mountains, etc. are governed by the five elements.

17. Wood is represented by everything upright, such as tall buildings, tall and thin trees, columns or pillars, etc.

18. Fire, denoting flames, is represented by pointed roofs, church spires, peaked mountains, etc.

19. Earth, generally flat, is represented by plateaus, flat roofs, etc.

20. Metal, round like coins, is represented by domed buildings, rounded hills, etc.

21. Water, with no shape, is generally shown in waves.

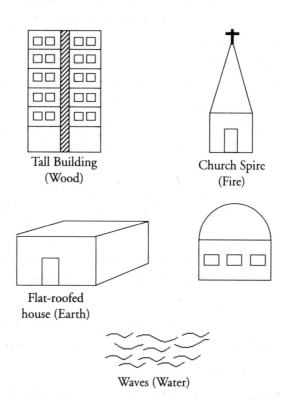

Tall Building
(Wood)

Church Spire
(Fire)

Flat-roofed
house (Earth)

Waves (Water)

Trigrams

1. Trigrams are arrangements of broken lines and solid lines in combinations of three.

2. There are eight trigrams in the study of Feng Shui.

3. Fu Hsi, the founder of the trigrams, noticed a tortoise, and after watching it for sometime, realised that the whole universe was mirrored in the methodical marking on the tortoise's shell. This sequence he called the 'Former Heaven Sequence', while the one which was rearranged 2,000 years later by King Wen and Duke Chou was called the 'Later Heaven Sequence'.

4. The evolution started with a simple yin and yang line.

Yang	Yin
Heaven	Creation

5. By adding one more line, we get four combinations

Winter	Summer
North	South

23

Autumn | Spring
West | East

——— —— —— | ————————
—— —— | ————————
———————— | ————————

6. By adding another line, we get eight possible combinations of three-lines each, with a special Chinese name tagged to each.

| Ch'ien |

————————
————————
————————

Heaven
North-West

| K'un |

—— ——
—— ——
—— ——

Creation
South-West

| Ken |

————————
—— ——
—— ——

Mountain
North-East

| Tui |

—— ——
————————
————————

Lake
West

| K'an |

—— ——
————————
—— ——

Water
North

| Li |

————————
—— ——
————————

Fire
South

| H'sun |

————————
————————
—— ——

| Chen |

—— ——
—— ——
————————

24

Wind	Thunder
South-East	East

7. These trigrams called Former Heaven Sequence, can be shown sequentially.

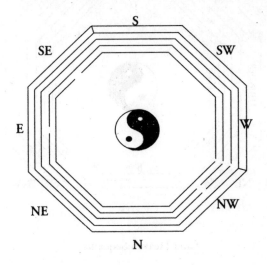

Former Heaven Sequence

8. The Former Heaven Sequence is normally found on mirrors and talismans to ward off evil sha.

9. The Later Heaven Sequence is found on the dial of the Chinese mariner's compass.

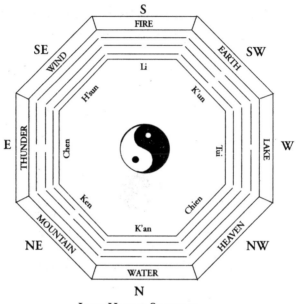

Later Heaven Sequence

10. The solid lines represent yang with its masculine attributes, while the broken lines are yin with its feminine attributes.

11. Chien, with its three solid lines, is the strong yang trigram, representing father, while K'un, with its three broken lines, is yin, representing mother.

Trigram	Symbol	Element	Person	Quality	Colour	Body Part	Season	Direction
☰	Heaven	Metal	Father	Authority	White	Head	Early Winter	North-West
☷	Earth	Earth	Mother	Nourishment	Black	Stomach	Early autumn	South-West
☳	Thunder	Wood	Elder son	Speed Roads	Green	Foot	Spring	East
☵	Water	Water	Middle son	Wheels Danger	Black	Ear	Winter	North
☶	Mountain	Earth	Youngest son	Obstacles	White	Hands	Early Spring	North-East
☴	Wind	Wood	Elder Daughter	Growth Food	Green	Buttock	Early Summer	South-East
☲	Fire	Fire	Middle Daughter	Fire	Red	Eyes	Summer	South
☱	Lake	Metal	Youngest Daughter	Joy	White	Mouth	Autumn	West

12. The eight trigrams with their attributes and symbolic occupations in specific areas can be shown tabularly.
13. Each trigram has its position fixed.
14. The name, qualities and symbolism of each trigram never change.
15. While the trigram with the three solid lines will always be ch'ien, symbolising authority, male and heaven, the trigram with the three broken lines will always be k'un, symbolising nourishment, female and earth.

Selection of Sites

1. Location of a house and its surroundings play a crucial role in Feng Shui.
2. Buildings, trees, ponds, rivers, mountains, hills, roads, lamp-posts, electric poles, etc., effect the flow of ch'i.
3. A successful business house nearby suggests that beneficial ch'i is flowing through the area, and hence one can safely select a site here.
4. While selecting the site, it is important to check the soil, the surroundings, the prosperity of neighbours, the shape of the land, and the health condi-tions of animals living in the vicinity.
5. The grass surrounding should be a healthy green which shows that ch'i is flowing freely.
6. Avoid a site which cannot nurture plants.
7. The soil on top should be fairly clean and porous and not sandy or wet.
8. An elevated site is always beneficial to the owner, with the back side higher than the front.

9. It would be ideal to have the rear portion facing higher ground or a hill, while the front faces lower ground or sea or valley.

10. A square or a rectangular plot is considered to be good.

11. In such a plot, the house should be located in the centre.

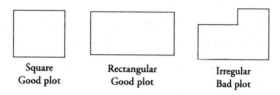

Square
Good plot

Rectangular
Good plot

Irregular
Bad plot

12. In a circular plot, a square house in the centre brings fortune and wealth.

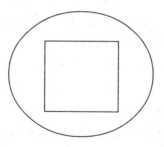

A circular plot with a square house

13. In a triangular plot, not considered to be good, you can ward off evil by avoiding fixing

30

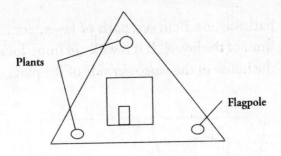

Plants

Flagpole

a door that faces any corner, and by placing a plant or flagpole to hide the corners.

14. Religious buildings are best suited to oval-shaped plots, since other buildings surround most of their boundary walls.

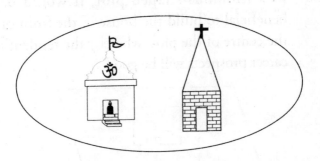

A religious building in an oval plot

15. In a plot which resembles a trapezoid, if the front is narrow, design a curve, either a curved

pathway, or a curved path of lawn, etc., in front of the house. If it is wider in front, locate the house in the narrower side of the plot.

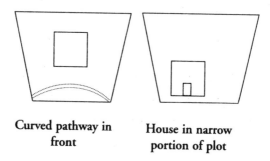

Curved pathway in front

House in narrow portion of plot

16. In a rhombus-shaped plot, it would be beneficial to build the house in the front or the centre of the plot, whereby the resident's career prospects will be good.

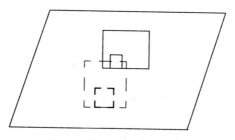

House in the centre or front of a rhombus-shaped plot

17. In a semicircular plot, considered to be very good, the ideal location for the house would be the centre of the plot.

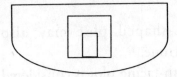

House in the centre in a semicircular plot

18. A rounded front or a back of a square or rectangular house would indicate growth or a balanced life, respectively.

19. Numerous problems crop up if you go in for a T-shaped plot.

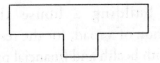

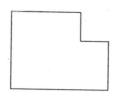

20. An L-shaped plot may also bring in misfortune.

21. A south-facing plot is considered to be good according to the Feng Shui system.

22. A house facing a large vacant or open space is deemed good, since the south winds in summer provide good, refreshing ventilation to the house.

ROADS

1. In Feng Shui, the layout of roads, and their direction are essential, as they carry the ch'i.

2. For a smooth and gentle flow of ch'i, the roads should follow natural contours and curve gently, whereas straight roads carry the ch'i quickly, thereby minimizing its effects.

3. Avoid building a house that faces a T-junction of a road, for the resident will be beset with health and financial problems.

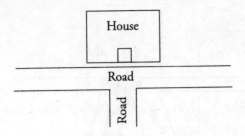

4. If your house is located at the dead end of a street, the ch'i effect will be weak, and the best cure would be to hang a mirror above the door, facing the road.

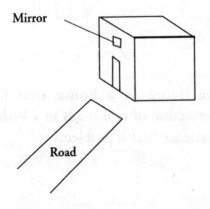

5. A house which faces two or more roads kills the ch'i, thus resulting in the resident always being on the defensive.

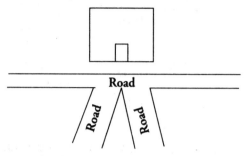

6. A road which curves sharply in front of the house slashes one's good fortune in business.

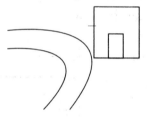

7. One living in a house that faces the intersection of two roads in a V-shape, will experience health problems.

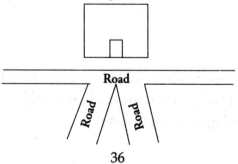

8. Shops with the entrance doors opening out to the road which has heavy traffic are ideally situated.

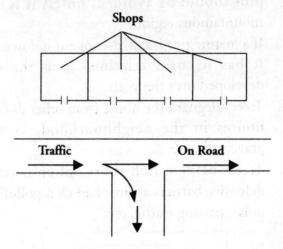

9. A corner shop whose door opens at the corner is good for maximum business.

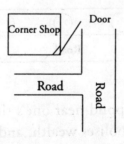

TREES

1. Tall and angular trees around the house or plot should be avoided, unless it is in a mountainous region.
2. If a mature tree is tall, do not cut it down, for it has its own relations with the ch'i developed over the years.
3. Trees safeguard the house from other ill-fated houses in the neighbourhood, as also graveyards, etc.
4. Trees, being a rich source of ch'i, act as defensive barriers against bad ch'i, pollution, noise, passing traffic, etc.

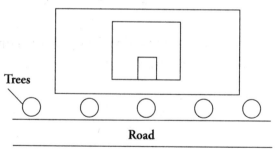

WATER BODY

A pool or pond near one's site is good, for water symbolises wealth, and attracts good ch'i to circulate.

Interior Structures

1. The interior structures also affect the flow of ch'i.
2. Doors and windows are the inlets and outlets through which ch'i circulates.
3. Staircases and corridors conduct ch'i from place to place.
4. Various kinds of furniture and furnishings, plants and interior doors guide ch'i through the rooms.

DOORS

1. The main door to the house should be in proportion to the house, neither too large (which allows harmful ch'i to invade) nor too small (which obstructs entry of ch'i).

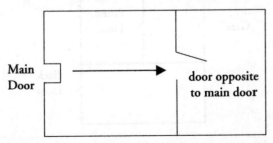

2. There should be nothing in front of the main door that obstructs free circulation of ch'i, no t even a wall.

3. The main door should open into a wide area inside the house, and not a narrow room or corridor.

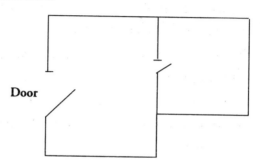

Door

4. Do not have the gate, the front door and the back door in a straight line, as this will allow ch'i to rush in and out, without circulating in the house.

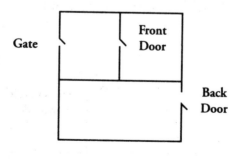

Gate

Front Door

Back Door

5. If the gate, main door and back door are aligned in a straight line, hang a wind chime in the front room, or a screen behind the front door, or in front of the back door.

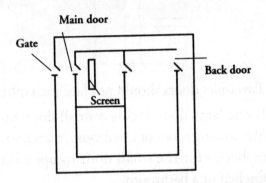

6. The direction of a door in the house brings in untold fortune, depending upon where each door is placed. For example,

South — fame and prosperity

East — wealth and finance

West — children achieving fame

North — good business and relationship

South-east— Wealth and finance

North-east— intelligence and educational success

North-west—travel and new ventures

South-west—peace and happiness

7. It is always good for doors to face each other directly.

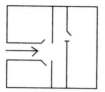

8. Two toilet doors should not face each other.

9. If one large door, facing a small door, opens into a living room or a bedroom, then it would be better for the small door to open into a kitchen or a bathroom.

10. Doors should be well oiled and free of any squeaks which would disturb ch'i.

WINDOWS

1. Windows should open outwards to allow good ch'i to circulate in the room.

2. One will be affected by broken glass panes of windows, and have troubles with one's ears, nose and eyes.
3. Windows should be in proportion to the door, else they will also allow evil ch'i to enter.

STAIRS

1. Ch'i flows up and down the stairs, hence their placement is important for Feng Shui.
2. They should be wide and well lit.
3. Do not have a staircase directly in front of the main door, for then sha sneaks in and good opportunities in life fade away.

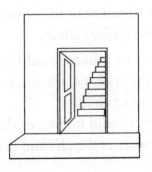

4. A gently curving staircase is the best for it allows ch'i to flow gently through the room and up the stairs.

43

5. Avoid building a staircase in the centre of the house.

BEAMS AND COLUMNS

1. Since the beam in a room carries the load of the room, and creates compression, it is advisable not to keep the bed or office furniture directly underneath it, for it causes health problems.

2. A beam over the head causes headaches, pain over the abdomen, disorders of the stomach, and swelling of the feet.

3. Where it is not possible to change the furniture for want of space, the remedial measure would be to fix a mirror in the beam, or to have a false ceiling.

4. Columns or pillars should be constructed within the wall, or in corners, to allow free movement of ch'i.

5. Columns should be free of sharp edges, for this imbalances the ch'i and deadens it.

Houses

1. The placement of each room in a house is important if one wants to live in harmony and happiness.
2. The furniture and furnishings also have to be placed in each room the Feng Shui way.

BEDROOM

1. The bedroom is the most important room in the house, for most of us spend one-third of our lives in it.
2. An ideal bedroom should be at the rear of the house, far from the main door.
3. The bed should ideally be placed in a corner of the room to enable one to have a wide view at one glance.
4. The bed should not be placed opposite the door.
5. The head of the bed should be towards the east.

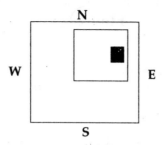

6. The bed should not face a window, and it would be best to have it against a solid wall.

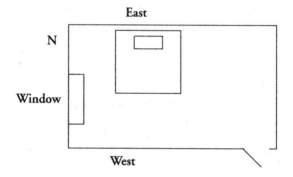

7. While it is good to have the bed on the east side of the bedroom for children, for adults the west would be best.

8. The bed should be placed in such a way that one can immediately see anyone entering the room.

9. The furniture around the room, few in fact, should be rounded so as to allow ch'i to flow freely.

10. Muted lighting and soft colours on the walls and furnishings will ensure peace and harmony.

LIVING ROOM

1. The living room, a common meeting place for family and friends, should be close to the entrance or main door.

2. It should be well lit, comfortable, and give a feeling of relaxation and security.

3. The furniture should be arranged along the sides of the walls, and not in the centre.

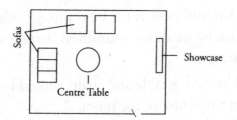

4. Avoid placing the sofa with its back to the windows or door, otherwise place a mirror in such a way so that the occupant of the sofa can

see in the mirror anyone entering or standing near a window.

5. Windows should open outwards.

6. Any sharp edges along the wall should be hidden by plants or wall hangings to soften the effect of the room.

7. For an irregularly shaped room, mirrors or plants act as buffers and ward off the evil.

8. Beams and rafters can be concealed by a false ceiling.

DINING ROOM

1. The dining room should not be visible from the main door, and if it is the case, a screen or a curtain can act as a barrier.

2. A round table is the best, though others can also be used, for roundness is suggestive of heaven.

3. The dining table and chairs should be placed in the centre of the room.

4. The guest of honour should be placed near the door.

5. Dining chairs should be in even numbers.

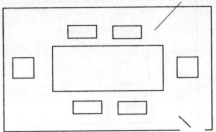

Guest of honour

KITCHEN

1. The kitchen, being a symbolic source of wealth, should be in the south-east or eastern side of the house.

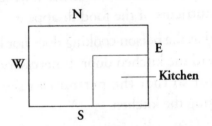

N

E

W

Kitchen

S

2. As the south represents fire, and the east represents wood, elements that are required in the kitchen, it would be ideal to have the kitchen in the south-east.

3. Do not place the stove near a sink or a refrigerator, as fire and water play against each other.

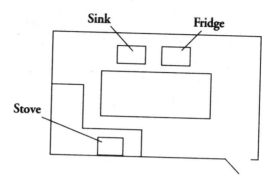

4. See that the kitchen and the stove do not face the main door.

5. Avoid a kitchen opposite a toilet.

6. Do not have the stove under a window, for the nutrients of the food disappear.

7. See that the person cooking does not have her back to the kitchen door. If necessary, hang a mirror so that the person can see who is entering the kitchen.

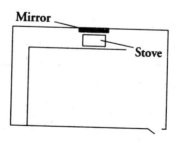

TOILET

1. The ideal place for a toilet is the north side of the house, as north represents the water element. A toilet in the south-east (prosperity) will flush away all wealth.

2. Brightly lit and well ventilated, the toilet should not be in front of the main door, for this will affect the resident's health and wealth.

3. All water conduits and drainpipes should be totally covered, for the Chinese believe that water that leaves the room should not be seen.

4. On entering, the toilet seat should not be visible. Hang a wind chime or a mirror over the seat to draw one's attention away from the seat.

5. Always keep the toilet door closed, and hang a

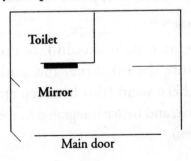

51

mirror on it, if the toilet is located in front of the main door.

6. A toilet can affect the family's health if it is situated at the end of a corridor. To counteract its ill-effects, place a mirror or wind chime outside the toilet.

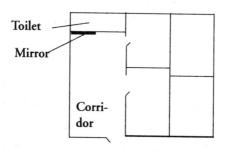

7. It is advisable not to have a toilet in the centre of the house, or opposite the main door.

Main Door

1. The main door should face the south, to capture the sunshine, and avoid the cold northern wind (this has been applicable to China, and hence integrated in the Feng Shui system).

2. Some Feng Shui experts would like to place the main door in accordance with one's time of birth.

3. Lo Shu also helps in deciding the location of the main door.

Lo Shu — The Magic Square

1. Feng Shui advocates the concept of space for which a mysterious diagram known as Lo Shu was first evolved in China.

2. Lo Shu is a square divided into nine compartments, each one representing a direction of the compass.

3. Numbers 1 to 9 are placed in such a way that by adding the numbers horizontally, vertically or diagonally, one gets the number 15.

4. Each of these numbers, except number 5, represents one of the eight directions and eight trigrams.

5. Each number has relevance to a basic element, a family member, colour, quality, and season, and has both yin and yang characters.

	S	
4	9	2
3	5	7
8	1	6

E (left)   W (right)   N (bottom)

1 K'an ☵ North
8 Ken ☶ North-east
3 Chen ☳ East
4 H'sun ☴ South-east
9 Li ☲ South
2 K'un ☷ South-west
7 Tui ☱ West
6 Ch'ien ☰ North-west

6. The Lo Shu, an old Chinese charm, lends its principles during construction of buildings, and has two formulas, one for males, and one for females.

CALCULATION FOR MALES

1. Subtract the last two numbers of the year of birth from 100.

2. Divide this by 9.
3. The remainder is Annual Number.
4. If there is no remainder, then 9 will be taken as the Annual Number.

For example,

Year of birth   1941

$$100 - 41 = 59$$
$$59 / 9 = 6$$

Remainder 5

So the main door should be placed in the south-west. (Refer to chart)

CALCULATION FOR FEMALES

1. Subract 4 from the last two number of the year of birth.
2. Divide this by 9.
3. The remainder is the Annual Number.
4. In the absence of a remainder, the Annual number will be 9.

For example,

Year of birth   1948

$$48 - 4 = 44$$
$$44 / 9 = 4$$

Remainder 8

So the main door should be in the north-east.

Chart Using Year of Birth

For Males	S	NE	W	NW	SW	SE	E	SW	N
Annual No.	9	8	7	6	5	4	3	2	1
YEAR OF BIRTH	1901	1902	1903	1904	1905	1906	1907	1908	1909
	1910	1911	1912	1913	1914	1915	1916	1917	1918
	1919	1920	1921	1922	1923	1924	1925	1926	1927
	1928	1929	1930	1931	1932	1933	1934	1935	1936
	1937	1938	1939	1940	1941	1942	1943	1944	1945
	1946	1947	1948	1949	1950	1951	1952	1953	1954
	1955	1956	1957	1958	1959	1960	1961	1962	1963
	1964	1965	1966	1967	1968	1969	1970	1971	1972
	1973	1974	1975	1976	1977	1978	1979	1980	1981
	1982	1983	1984	1985	1986	1987	1988	1989	1990
	1991	1992	1993	1994	1995	1996	1997	1998	1999
Annual No.	6	7	8	9	1	2	3	4	5
For Females	NW	W	NE	S	N	SW	E	SE	NW

5. While many Feng Shui experts base the main door placement using the year of birth, others use the time of birth, using elements and Chinese animals related to the element.

Chart Using Time of Birth

Animal	Element	Time of Birth	Direction
Rat	Water	11 pm— 1am	N
Ox	Earth	1 am — 3 am	N,NE
Tiger	Wood	3 am — 5 am	E,NE
Rabbit	Wood	5 am — 7 am	E
Dragon	Earth	7 am — 9 am	E,SE
Snake	Fire	9 am — 11 am	SE,S
Horse	Fire	11 am—1 pm	S
Goat	Earth	1 pm —3 pm	S,SW
Monkey	Metal	3 pm —5 pm	W,SW
Cock	Metal	5 pm —7 pm	W
Dog	Earth	7 pm —9 pm	W,NW
pig	Water	9 pm —11 pm	N,NW

6. According to Feng Shui, the main door should be larger than the inner doors, and both should open in the same direction.

GARDEN

1. The Chinese believe that the bounderies of the house are guarded by four animals - a red

57

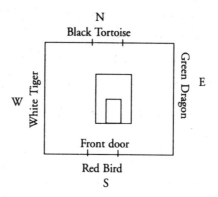

bird, a white tiger, a black tortoise, and a green dragon — which represent the west, north, south and east respectively.

2. The black tortoise, or the back garden, should be more elevated than the red bird, or the front garden.

3. The back garden should be larger than the front one, to shield the inmates of the house.

4. A garden sloping upwards to the main door in front of the house should be avoided since this will bring financial loss or family discord.

5. The garden at the back should not slope away from the back door, for this indicates that good business dealings will dwindle and fade away.

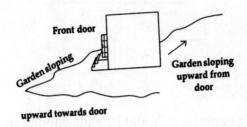

6. The right side garden, representing the green dragon, should be slightly higher than the left which represents the white tiger.

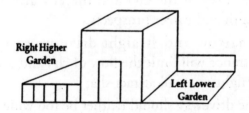

7. The green dragon and that white tiger should be well balanced, otherwise one would become more harmful, causing untold miseries to the occupant.

8. An L-shaped building, considered not good, can be amended by planting a tree in the missing corner.

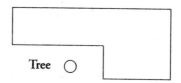

Tree ○

ENTRANCE

1. The entrance should be wide enough to allow the good ch'i easy access to the house.

2. Any obstructions like a pole, a tree, a column, a pillar, etc., should be removed if they are in front of the entrance, obstructing the entry of the ch'i and thereby affecting health and career prospects.

3. A narrow and straight drive-way to the entrance will limit the flow of ch'i and a very straight one will attract sha.

4. The driveway should neither be too wide nor too narrow, but should be in proportion to the width of the gate.

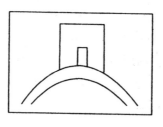

5. Ideally, it would be best to have a gently curving path to the entrance.

6. A driveway that runs along a side of the house will encourage the ch'i to hug the pathway and avoid the house, thus leaving it lifeless.

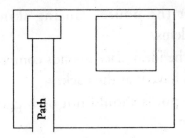

7. Too wide a pathway towards the house will weaken one's career and financial prospects.

8. A path narrower than the main door will bring bad luck to the inmates.

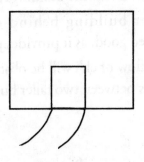

POOL

1. Feng Shui recommends a swimming pool or a pond if space permits.

2. It would be better to have it a little distance away from the main entrance, otherwise misfortune can occur, and excess of yin may enter the house, causing skin and lung problems.

3. But the ideal place in one's compound would be to have it at the back.

4. The pools should not be bigger than the house.

5. The water should always be kept clean to discourage sha, and thereby ill-health.

THE BUILDING

1. The height of the building should be in consonance with the buildings around.

2. A higher building behind one's own is considered good, as it provides protection.

3. Smooth flow of ch'i will be obstructed if one's house lies between two taller buildings.

4. A square, round or rectangular house is good, but the best is the first two, for they represent earth and heaven.

5. In a U-shaped house, which is considered unlucky for marriage, you can offset the ill-effects by planting a row of flowering plants or shrubs.

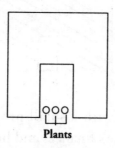

Plants

6. An extended arm to the left or right of the house could affect one's health.

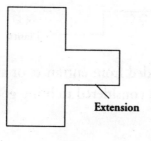

Extension

7. Projections from both south-west and north-east, are better to be avoided, while those in the north-west and south-east are good.

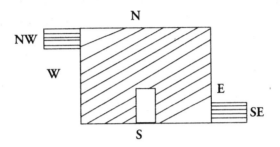

8. A house with a small projecting entrance affects one's finances and health. This can be offset by planting flowers on either side.

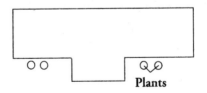

Plants

9. A rounded front entrance, or a rounded back door, is considered to bring good fortune.

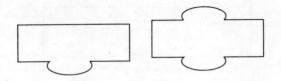

10. Triangular projections on the sides are unhealthy.

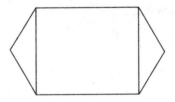

11. A house with a front entrance leading diagonally to either side is good, so long as there is no door on the diagonal sides.

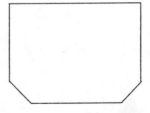

12. A T-shaped house is good so long as the shaft of the T is not longer than the width of the bar.

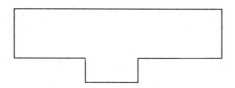

13. A house which has extension on all sides, resembling a cross, will bring loss of property to the owner.

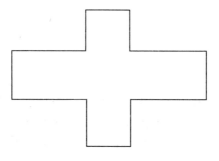

Offices, Shops and Factories

1. Feng Shui provides ways to always have an edge over competitors.
2. By changing the office according to Feng Shui principles, one's business prospects brighten.

OFFICE

1. The director's room, situated in a most commanding position in the building, should be in a corner, away from the entrance.
2. There should be ample space leading to his room, for this allows ch'i to move around freely.
3. Avoid having the room at the end of a long and dark corridor which will result in weak management.
4. It is better to have the director's room on a higher floor, room on a higher floor, and on a higher level than the toilet.
5. The director's room should have a ceiling which is higher than those in other rooms.

6. Square or rectangular offices are good while L-shaped ones create problems.

7. In a rectangular office room the length should be slightly more than the breadth.

8. It is advisable not to hang a light, a plant or any other object over the desk.

9. Projecting corners can be softened by placing plants there.

10. The desk should be in a corner, away from the door, with the occupant seated facing the door.

11. A solid wall rather than a window behind the desk would offer protection and create stability in business.

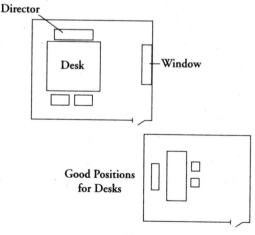

Director

Desk

Window

Good Positions for Desks

12. One who sits close to the door will have a tendency to leave the office early, and in order to motivate one to work longer, a mirror can be placed on the opposite wall, through which one can view the door.

13. When two people occupy a room, it would be best to have them both facing the door.

14. The desk should be placed parallel to the wall,

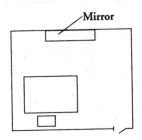

and not too close to the corner.

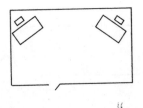

15. The desk should be neither too large nor too small.

16. Square and rectangular desks are suitable for commercial business.

17. Round, oval or curved tables are suitable for creative work.

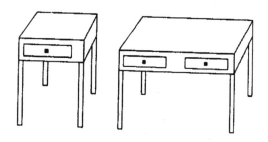

18. It would be considered best to have soft colours rather than bright colours for the

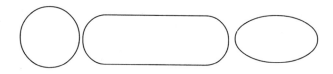

furniture.

19. Plants, flowerpots, vases, paintings, and an aquarium bring in prosperity to the office.

20. Plants, signifying longevity, should be placed behind the desk for a good flow of ch'i.

21. Lighting should create pleasantness and balance, without being too dim or too harshly bright.

22. The rooms should be well ventilated.

23. The accounts room with its cash counter should be in the centre of the building or in a quiet place to encourage good business.

24. The computer, which brightens and improves ch'i movement, should be so placed that the operator sits facing the door.

25. The phone should be beside the computer.

SHOPS

1. The entrance of the shop should not face the corner of another building.

2. The entrance of the shop should not be opposite a narrow gap between two

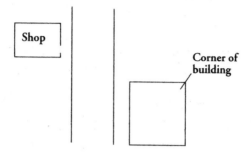

buildings, as this may lead to loss of business.

3. The entrance of the shop should not lead

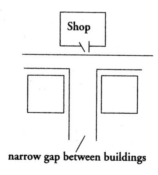

narrow gap between buildings

straight into a corridor.

4. The door should not be too big to attract an overdose of ch'i nor too small to keep it away.

5. The cash counter should not be parallel to the

door.

FACTORIES

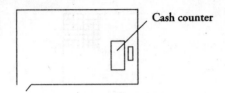

Cash counter

1. The Feng Shui principles for shops and offices apply to factories too.

2. Since storage requires more space, the application of Feng Shui in factories depends on the working of the unit.

3. For drill machines, rotating machineries, etc., the unit should be placed in the north of the premises.

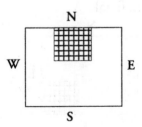

4. For storage of goods, security gate, etc., the north-east is ideal.

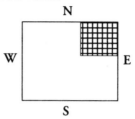

5. For despatch, transport and work in progress, the east is suitable.

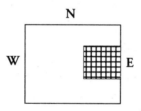

6. For labour-intensive jobs, the south-east proves beneficial.

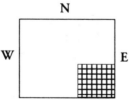

7. For heating purposes, furnaces, etc., the south is ideal.

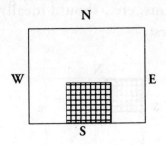

8. For biological process, use the south-west.

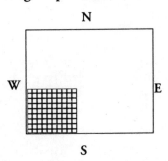

9. The west would be ideal for recreation.

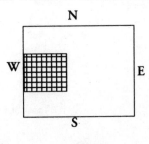

10. Canteen, management, intial process design, rest rooms, etc., should ideally be in the north-west.

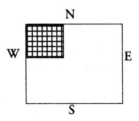

Ba-gua and Cures

1. Ba-gua is a grid, or a map, in the shape of an octagon, divided into eight directions, eight life directions and eight life situations. It is also called 'Later Heaven Sequence'.

1. South	Li	Fire	Prosperity and fame
2. South-east	H'sun	Wind	Wealth and money
3. East	Chen	Thunder	Family and health
4. North-east	Ken	Mountain	Knowledge
5. North	K'an	Water	Career
6. North-west	Ch'ien	Heaven	Helpful associates
7. West	Tui	Lake	Progeny
8. South-west	K'un	Earth	Marriage

SOUTH (FIRE)

1. The trigram for fire consists of a solid line above and below a broken line, appearing like a flame.

2. The house for the fire symbolises light and clarity.

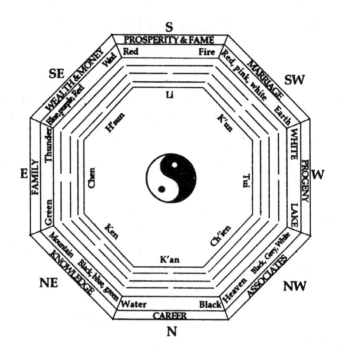

3. Just as a light shines within when one's end
    draws near, likewise this house is illumined
    from within and illuminates others.

4. When the ba-gua of this house is strong
    (projecting on this area), people in this house
    achieve fame, and when absent, their
    confidence will be undermined by the
    influence of others.

SOUTH-EAST (WINE)

1. The trigram for wind consists of two solid lines above a broken line.

2. The house for wind reveals a perpetual flow of good fortune and wealth.

3. Wind symbolises promotion at work, recognition of meretoious work and appreciation by colleagues.

4. With a strong ba-gua fortune will flow in smoothly but a weak one will result in frequent accidents and hampering in legal contracts leading to losses.

EAST (THUNDER)

1. The trigram for thunder consists of a solid line below two broken lines.

2. Thunder symbolises the rise of a solid powerful force which fades away harmlessly.

3. The house for thunder denotes occupation by elders, like the parents, the boss, the director, etc.

4. A strong ba-gua of this house indicates great success in life, while a weak one leads to loss of energy, and listlessness.

NORTH-EAST (MOUNTAIN)

1. The trigram for mountain consists of a solid line above two broken lines, giving the appearance of a cave in a mountain.

2. The house for mountain represents meditation and prayers, and the inner knowledge of a person.

3. The ba-gua of this house should be well balanced.

4. A strong ba-gua leads to discord and tension in the family, encouraging selfish motives, and a weak one will deprive a couple of any issue or offspring.

NORTH (WATER)

1. The trigram for water consists of a solid line in between two broken lines.

2. The house for water represents good career opportunites where one has the freedom to take decisions for a harmonious life.

3. With a strong ba-gua, there will be a lot of wealth that will be utilised beneficially, while a weak one may bring ill-health to someone in the house.

NORTH-WEST (HEAVEN)

1. The trigram for heaven consists of three solid lines.

2. The creative force, called 'Helpful friends', stimulates and nourishes the soil with plenty of sunshine, rain, and other atmospheric forces.

3. The house for heaven denotes good friends and neighbours, and a supportive staff.

4. A strong ba-gua encourages the residents to be supportive of people less privileged financially, and a weak one will lead to the person facing problems with his employees.

West (Lake)

1. The trigram for lake has two solid lines below a broken line, appearing like waves or ripples over a lake.

2. The house for lake symbolises creativity in projects, art etc., bringing in children and a youthful joy.

3. A strong ba-gua indicates happiness and a good social life, while the person will find it difficult to economise, and therefore be denied enjoyment.

South-west (Earth)

1. The trigram for earth consists of three broken lines.

2. The house for earth stands for good relationship in marriage and among family members.

3. A strong ba-gua indicates women's happiness is more than that of men, and a weak one

may result in the womenfolk facing troubles, and difficulties in land issues.

APPLICATION OF BA-GUA

1. Being octagonal in shape, the ba-gua can be applied or superimposed on furniture, a room, a house, land, etc.

2. The ba-gua can also be superimposed on a palm or face to read a person's destiny.

3. The application of the ba-gua refers to a method called 'The Three-Door Gate of Ch'i'.

4. The front door plays a vital role in the application of the ba-gua.

5.   The front door is the entrance through which ch'i enters the house for harmony, peace and happiness.

6. There are three possible ways the front door can open:

- If the door opens in the centre, then it represents career.

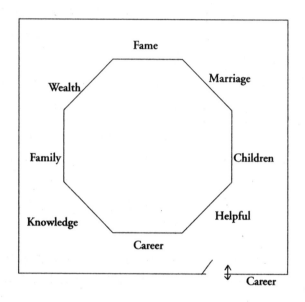

- If the door opens to the right side of the wall, then helpful people are denoted.
- If the door opens to the left side of the wall, then knowledge is indicated.

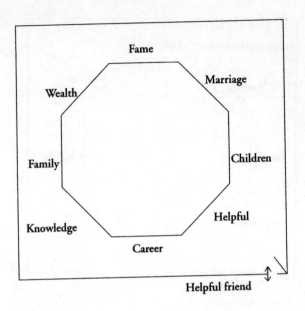

Helpful friend

7. Every door in the house creates another ba-gua.

8. The ba-gua for a new floor begins where the top step meets the floor level.

9. Each room also has its own bagua.

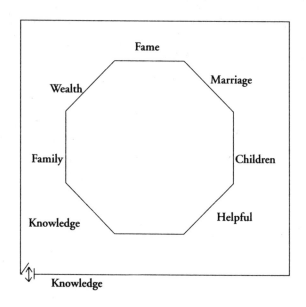

10. In an irregularly shaped house, the missing space called the negative space, can be extended to counteract illeffects. Or, hang a mirror, a wind chime, a crystal ball or plant a creeper there.

For example, if a room has a corner, which denotes wealth, missing, then the person will be beset with financial problems, and hence he can enhance the ba-gua by hanging any one of the items mentioned above.

11. Similarly, in the corner of an office room, that is reserved for fame, keep a pot of red flowers. It will lead to the person's promotion to a higher post.

CURES

1. There are eight basic cures-mirrors, light, plants, water, crystal balls, wind chimes, flutes and colours.

2. These cures help enhancing or adjusting the ba-gua of a room, improve the circulation of ch'i freely, and balance the irregularities in the house.

3. Before installing the cures, the area should be thoroughly cleaned of all debris, cobweb, dirt, dust, etc.

Mirrors

1. Mirrors are used as a remedial measure to deflect evil spirits, and encourage the flow of ch'i.

2. By hanging a mirror at the edge of the wall of the negative or missing space, the area appears like a projection, and hence balance is achieved.

3. One should avoid a mirror in the bedroom, so that ch'i can be funneled and guided gently round the room.

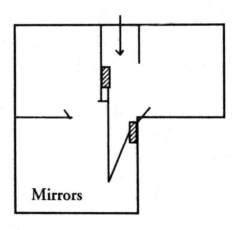

Mirrors

4. When doors within a house are badly aligned, the ill-effect can be rectified by placing a mirrorappropriately.

5. When a door is fixed at the end of a corridor, which leads to health problems and obstruction in career progress, hang a mirror over the door.

6. It is better not to place a mirror opposite a bed, for the Chinese believe the soul leaves the body for a few hours while sleeping, and an image of it in the mirror might disturb it.

7. In a shop, install a mirror behind the cash counter to increase profits.

8. A mirror placed behind a showcase in a shop doubles the amout of display, creating depth in the room.

9. Avoid the entrance to the shop facing a mirror, for this will encourage sha to enter the shop.

10. The mirror used for encouraging good ch'i to circulate freely should be placed at an angle, while the one used for deflecting sha should be parallel to the wall, on which it is hung.

11. A mirror should be free of dust and damage.

12. Two mirrors should not be placed side by side.

LIGHT

1. Light, which is a symbol of the sun denoting energy, enlivens the area of the ba-gua, in which it is placed.

2. In an L-shaped building, a light at the missing corner balances the ba-gua.

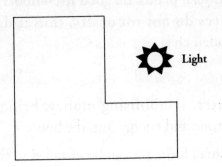

Light

3. Soft lighting is better than the harsh glare of overbright bulbs.

PLANTS

1. Plants, symbolising nature and growth, enhances ch'i in the room of ba-gua.

2. When placed in a corner, they help ch'i to circulate well.

3. Plants in sharp corners ward off evil effects.

4. Flowerpots on large window sills control the rushing ch'i.

5. Artificial plants are good for indoors as their leaves do not rot or dry, thus it does not deaden ch'i.

WATER

1. Water, symbolising money, brings good fortune and energy into the house.

2. A small fountain can be installed in the front room of a house, or in the foyer of an office, thus acctivating the bagua there.

3. A fish aquarium near the cash counter of a shop or a restaurant fetches plenty of money. It can be installed in a house or an office also, as it normally absorbs all impurities the room.

CRYSTAL BALLS

1. Crystal balls symbolising positive energy, bring good fortune, by enchancing the bagua position and ch'i of the house.

2. As reflectors of light, they covert the ominous ch'i to a positive one.

3. They help in the free circulation of ch'i in the house.

4. Small crystals, used instead of the precious and unaffordable diamonds, are better suited than large ones.

WIND CHIMES

1. Wind chimes, symbolising harmony, enhance the ba-gua of a house, by controlling the flow of ch'i.

2. They act as shields against sha's entry in a house.

3. In a house where the main door faces the back door, a wind chime hung in a proper place in between the doors, moderates the flow of ch'i.

4. In long corridors having numerous doors, wind chimes are useful.

FLUTES

1. Flutes, mainly made of bamboo, enchances the effect of ch'i.

2. In a house where the ceiling is low, or the beam is exposed, two flutes tied with a red ribbon are placed,mouths downwards, making a 45 degree angle beneath the ceiling or beam, creating a ba-gua formation. This helps the ch'i flowing thrugh the flutes to rise upward and circulate.

3. They also ward off evil effects, and bring peace, stability and safety.

4. When a flute is played, the weak ch'i is driven away to be replaced by a strong one.

5. When the flute is shaken, evil spirits are driven away.

COLOURS

1. Colours symbolise harmony and balance, thus strengthening one's destiny.

2. Colours stimulate one's mind, effciency at work, and one's health.

3. Red, the colour of the fire element, symbolises fame, good fortune, prosperity and strength.

4. Red colour should be used adequately, but excessive use will create difficulties.

5. The use of red in the dining room or kitchen will help one to digest food well.

6. Yellow, symbolising energy and brightness, brings fame, progress and power.

7. Yellow in the living room helps in socialising pleasantly, and establishing good relationship.

8. White, symbolising purity, is feared by the Chinese, and it used sparingly, except in some buildings.

9. Green, symbolising tranquility and freshness, brings good health, growth and progress.

10. A combination of red and greens is considered good and fortunate.